There's Something Better Than Going to Heaven

To: Delanie
From: Dr. Bailey

William D. Bailey, M.D.

CrossHouse

Published by
CrossHouse Publishing
PO Box 461592
Garland, Texas 75046-1592
www.crosshousepublishing.org
1-877-212-0933

Copyright William D. Bailey 2008
All Rights Reserved

Printed in the United States of America
by Lightning Source, LaVergne, TN
Cover design by Dennis Davidson

ISBN 978-1-934749-08-1
Library of Congress Control Number: 2007939867

TO ORDER ADDITIONAL COPIES FOR $9.95 EACH
(ADD $3 SHIPPING FOR FIRST BOOK,
50 CENTS FOR EACH ADDITIONAL BOOK)
CONTACT CROSSHOUSE PUBLISHING
PO BOX 461592
GARLAND, TX 75046-1592
www.crosshousepublishing.org
877-212-0933 (toll-free)

TABLE OF CONTENTS

Introduction
Page 17

Chapter 1
Be a Great Commission Christian
Page 21

Chapter 2
My Commissioning to Share
Page 23

Chapter 3
Training for the Great Commission
Page 26

Chapter 4
Prayer
Page 30

Chapter 5
Church Visitation
Page 35

Chapter 6
The Gideons
Page 38

Chapter 7
Prison Ministry
Page 42

Chapter 8
Mission Trips Abroad
Page 48

Chapter 9
Personal Witnessing in the Work Place
Page 57

Chapter 10
Sharing Jesus Without Fear
Page 62

Chapter 11
Spiritual Warfare
Page 64

Chapter 12
Is Heaven Real?
Page 68

Chapter 13
Drinking from my Saucer
Page 71

Appendix
Page 75

Unless otherwise indicated, all Scriptures are from the King James Version of the Bible.

FOREWORD

William D. Bailey, M.D. is truly a Great Commission Christian. His first book, *You Will Never Run Out of Jesus*, revealed how he surrendered his life to Jesus at an early age. He mentioned at the beginning of that book how I had a small part in leading him to Christ during a revival at his home church in Hunter, LA. I am honored and humbled that he asked me to write the foreword for his second book: *There's Something Better Than Going to Heaven*.

Dr. Bailey knew that God had a plan for his life. He wanted to be a doctor and succeeded admirably in his studies as a student, intern, and surgery resident. He practiced medicine successfully for 25 years before retiring from active practice. He continues to work in emergency rooms in north Louisiana to help finance his mission projects.

Dr. Bailey had a deep and abiding conviction that God wanted him to use the second half of his life as a volunteer and medical missionary. He received the symbolic commissioning as a Great Commission Christian when his pastor baptized him in the Jordan River. He and his wife, Vickie, have traveled all over the world with fellow doctors, nurses, dentists, pastors, evangelists, and Christian friends sharing the good news that Jesus saves.

At the various mission sites, sick people come in large numbers for healing of their bodies. When they meet Dr. Bill, they meet a man who is concerned not only with their physical illnesses but also with their souls! His EvangeCube is just as handy as his stethoscope. He and his team of volunteers have led literally thousands to the Lord. These experiences are chronicled in *You Will Never Run Out of Jesus*, a book that is a must-read for every Christian.

In this new book, Dr. Bailey states: "There's something better than going to heaven." That's an eye-opening title, isn't it? The answer is simple: "It's taking someone with you." As you read these pages, you will feel this doctor's compassion for lost souls. His heart burns within him as he teaches fellow believers that each of us has been commanded to "go and make disciples of all nations."

Warren Wiersbe said:

> Christianity is a missionary faith. The very nature of God demands this, for God is love and is not willing that any should perish (2 Pet. 3:9). Our Lord's death on the cross was for the whole world. If we are the children of God and share in his nature, then we will want to tell the good news to a lost world.
> *Be Loyal: Following the King of Kings*,
> Cook Communications: Colorado Springs, 1984, p. 214

The Apostle Paul defines the gospel in 1 Corinthians 15:3-4 as: "For I delivered unto you first of all that which I also received, how that Christ died for our sins according to the scriptures; And that He was buried, and that He rose again the third day according to the scriptures."

J. Vernon McGee said:

> Before any individual attempts to witness, he must first have an unshakable conviction for the truth of the Resurrection. He must have it settled in his own mind that Christ died for our sins and was buried, and Christ rose again. ... Then with these convictions, he can "go quickly and tell." My friend, you and I are to *go* and to *tell*.
>
> *Through the Bible With J. Vernon McGee*,
> Vol. IV, Thomas Nelson: Nashville, 1983, p. 152

We Christians need to do a better job of discipling new believers.

The purpose of *There's Something Better Than Going to Heaven*... is to teach (disciple) us in various ways we can share our faith in our Jerusalem: in our churches, homes, community, jobs, and civic clubs. Dr. Bailey shares effective experiences he has had in various areas of his life. He also presents excellent ways of witnessing through FAITH and the EvangeCube. He teaches us how we can have power through prayer and how to overcome fear in witnessing.

Dr. Bailey says, "God doesn't call us to be successful; he calls us to be faithful." The book closes with a beautiful reassurance that "I'm Drinking From My Saucer Because My Cup Has Overflowed!" Dr. Bailey is an excellent writer and shares many personal experiences with the reader. Those experiences constitute the strength of his writings. He doesn't ask us to do anything that he hasn't done himself. Did you know there's something better than going to heaven ... and that's taking someone with you!

Charles L. Foxworth, Ph.D.

DEDICATION

I dedicate this book to my parents,
William Joseph and Esther Bailey,
who insisted I get a proper education

and then provided the means and support

for me to obtain it.

Acknowledgments

I want to thank Dr. Charles Foxworth for two things. First, he was the visiting preacher at our church in Hunter, Louisiana, when I accepted Jesus as Lord and Savior.

On a Sunday afternoon following revival services at my church, he took me up to a front bedroom and told me about the saving grace of Jesus Christ. Right then and there I accepted Jesus. That night I went forward and made my decision public. That was a day I will never forget; it has eternal implications.

Dr. Charles Foxworth and his wife, Lois. Dr. Foxworth was the guest preacher when I accepted Jesus as my Savior in 1952.

I had lost contact with him over the years when my first cousin, Betty Carpenter, told me Dr. Foxworth was living in Ruston, LA. I learned he had retired from Louisiana Tech University where he had been the Director of Graduate Studies in Education and a professor of Curriculum, Instruction, and Leadership (1971-1996) and that he still preaches in various churches from time to time. I called long distance information and got his number and renewed an acquaintance from many years ago. I sent him a copy of my book, *You Will Never Run Out of Jesus*, and he really liked it. I sent him a rough copy of this book and, at my request, he contributed some very valuable input into the manuscript.

I also want to thank my wife, Vickie, for once again helping me with the manuscript; she was a valuable asset on my first book also. She continues to be a very supportive wife on all my Great Commission projects.

Thanks also to Katie Welch for encouraging me to proceed with my second book when I mentioned it soon after publishing my first, and thanks to the editor on this project, Deborah Davies.

INTRODUCTION

God wants all of us to be Great Commission Christians.

To be a Great Commission Christian you must first be a born-again Christian. Have you accepted Jesus as your one and only Savior? That is the *sine qua non* (absolute prerequisite) if you want to be a Great Commission Christian. You must admit you are a sinner and want forgiveness. Then you must accept Jesus as the Lord and Savior of your life. After that you should be so happy that you are a born-again Christian that you want to tell the world what Jesus has done for you. You will want to go and share the meaning of John 3:16 with everyone:

> *"For God so loved the world, that he gave His only begotten Son, that whosoever believeth in Him shall not perish, but have eternal life."*

Over a period of three years, Jesus taught his disciples, showing them that he was who he said he was. He died in the process. After he was resurrected by his Father, he then commanded them to go and make disciples of all the nations (Matt. 28:19-20). In fact, that command was made not only to the disciples, but also to all Christians.

Have you ever led someone to pray the sinner's prayer and accept Jesus as Lord and Savior? Although we ourselves can't save anyone, we can invite them to accept the one and only way to heaven. In John 16:6, Jesus says: "I am the way, the truth, and the life; no man cometh unto the Father, but by me."

It is our job to share the good news of our Savior. And what is it that we need to share? Four simple truths:

1. LIFE IS IN THE GOSPEL.
"For I am not ashamed of the gospel of Christ: for it is the power of God unto salvation unto everyone that believeth" (Rom. 1:16).

2. EVERYONE NEEDS SALVATION.
"For all have sinned, and come short of the grace of God" (Rom. 3:23).

"For the wages of sin is death; but the gift of God is eternal life through Jesus Christ our Lord" (Rom. 6:23).

3. SALVATION IS PROVIDED.
"But God commendeth his love toward us, in that, while we were yet sinners, Christ died for us" (Rom. 5:8).

4. SALVATION MUST BE ACCEPTED.
"That if thou shall confess with thy mouth the Lord Jesus and shall believe in thine heart that God hath raised him from the dead, thou shalt be saved" (Rom. 10:9).

"For whosoever shall call upon the name of the Lord shall be saved" (Rom. 10:13).

God has not called us to be successful; he has called us to be faithful. As a witness you cannot fail. You see, success is not measured by anyone's response; it is found in the sharing itself!

Once you have shared, only then can you pray that your witness is accepted and bears fruit. When your witness does come to fruition, the prayer you lead someone in can be as simple as:

> *Dear God, I know I am a sinner, and I confess that I have sinned against you. I believe that your Son Jesus died on a cross to pay for my sins, and that you raised him from the dead. I want to put my faith only in Jesus. Please forgive me and save me from my sins. I know that Jesus is Lord. Thank you for your gift of eternal life. I pray in Jesus' name. Amen.*

When you experience the privilege of leading someone in prayer to receive Jesus, you can celebrate with all of heaven. What a feeling! It is contagious.

You may ask why I'm so passionate about sharing the Good News. The answer is straightforward: It is because I serve a great Savior and am proud to share him with others. Jesus paid it all when he died on the cross for you and me ... and by his blood I am saved! It is my commission to tell others.

The following chapters will show you how I have accepted the order to *"Go tell."*

Chapter 1
Be a Great Commission Christian

*God never calls us to be successful;
he calls us to be faithful.*

There is something better than going to heaven ... and that is taking someone with you. In my previous book, *You Will Never Run Out of Jesus*, I described many of my journeys, mostly on the international mission field. In this book there is so much more to share with you about fulfilling the Great Commission. Listen to the words of Jesus:

> *And Jesus came and spake unto them, saying, All power is given unto me in heaven and in earth. Go ye therefore, and teach all nations, baptizing them in the name of the Father, and of the Son, and of the Holy Ghost: Teaching them to observe all things whatsoever I have commanded you: and, lo, I am with you always, even unto the end of the world. Amen.*
> Matthew 28: 18-20

To believers, Jesus said, "Go!" This is a *command*, not merely a statement, by Jesus just prior to his ascension into heaven. These were the last words he would utter on this Earth, and he used those final crucial moments to tell us what our job is.

Contrary to what some may think, the work he has given us doesn't necessarily have to take us far from home. There is just as much excitement and joy in local evangelism as there is in international evangelism. Wherever you present the gospel, it's the same indescribable thrill when someone responds by accepting Jesus as his or her Savior. As Luke 15:10 states: "Likewise, I say unto you, there is joy in the presence of the angels of God over one sinner that repenteth." James, the half-brother of Jesus, said: "Let him know, that he which converteth the sinner from the error of his way shall save a soul from death, and shall hide a multitude of sins" (Jas. 5:20).

This book lays out many methods you can use to present God's plan for salvation. In these chapters you will find the *very best method* I know to share the Good News, giving you the advantage of my experience sharing the gospel with thousands of others in a number of different situations and settings.

CHAPTER 2
My Commissioning to Share

I asked Jesus to let his will be mine.

In December 1998, my wife, Vickie, and I were privileged to go to Israel on a tour of the Holy Land with evangelist Mike Gilchrist. On the way to Israel we met two couples who have become our lifelong friends: Charles and Gayle Laughridge and Ty and Beth Tyner.

One night while we were eating supper together in Tiberias, Ty said he wanted to share with us why he felt compelled to return to the Holy Land a second time. He told us that while he was visiting the Garden of Gethsemane the previous year listening to Rev. Gilchrist give a sermon, something astounding had happened. Jesus appeared in front of him. As clear as day, Jesus pointed to him and said, "Go witness for me." Ty said he has not been the same since. Every day that he doesn't tell at least 10 people about Jesus, he is miserable.

There was not a dry eye at the table.

I couldn't get the story off my mind all evening. I thought that if Jesus could change Ty so much, he could change me too. As I prayed that night, I confessed to God that, while I knew I was his child from my previous salvation experience, I now realized I had not been a true servant. I asked him to let his will be mine. I wanted to surrender my life and services to him ... no matter what that entailed. "Just show me the way," I prayed.

Over the next year, my life was changed forever. When we truly place ourselves in his service, things indeed do change. That next year, after almost 25 years of private medical practice, I retired and dedicated myself to frequent medical missions abroad to tell the world about Jesus. I also made plans to return to the Holy Land. Intrigued by the place that had changed so many lives, including Ty's and mine, I felt compelled to return there in May 2000.

From left: Donnie Gilchrist, Dr. Damon Vaughn (my pastor), Vickie (my wife), and Rev. Mike Gilchrist stop for a photo near the baptism site on the Jordan River in the Holy Land.

This time I had something special in mind. As part of a commissioning service in the land where a year and a half before I had promised to pursue the Great Commission, I wanted to be baptized in the Jordan River, the place where Christ himself accepted his Father's commission. A number of people joined us on the trip, including my pastor, Dr. Damon Vaughn, and his wife, Carolyn. When we finally arrived at the

Jordan River, we found a baptismal site just below the dam where water usually empties from the Sea of Galilee into the river. Most important, it was only a few miles upriver from where Jesus was baptized.

Because of the dry season, the river was barely flowing. The air that day was cool, but the water itself was downright chilly. When Dr. Vaughn asked me about why I wanted to be baptized when I had already been baptized years before, I was glad for the chance to tell him that I wanted to seal my promise to God to be a Great Commission Christian — and that I could imagine no better place than to do so than in the Jordan River.

I was glad Dr. Vaughn and I didn't have to wait long in the water. While Dr. Vaughn baptized me in 3 and a half feet of cold water on that memorable afternoon, Vickie snapped a photo or two to commemorate what I considered one of the most sacred events of my life.

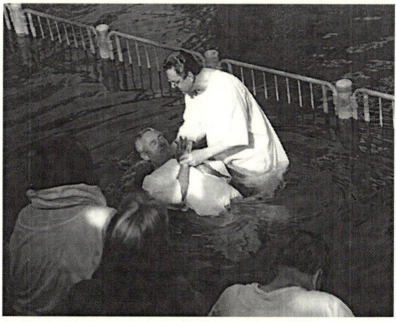

Dr. Vaughn baptizes me in the Jordon River on May 6, 2000.

CHAPTER 3
Training for the Great Commission

Simply put, the EvangeCube is the most effective evangelical tool I have ever utilized.

In the time since I became a Christian in 1952, I had never taken the Great Commission seriously, which, unfortunately, is an attitude shared by many. Although I probably would have had many opportunities during high school, college, medical school, my training as a surgery resident, and during my 24 years in private practice, I never really witnessed directly to others. Sure, I went along on church visitation night, but I never presented the gospel for salvation purposes; I merely issued invitations to come to church.

That changed when in January 2000 I visited Rev. Billy Pierce in the hospital and told him of my plan to make medical mission trips all over the world. He encouraged me to get appropriate training in evangelism and recommended the FAITH course he himself had taken. Billy said the course had transformed his personal evangelizing, and he emphasized his point by saying that if I had to go out of state to take the course, then to do so because it was that important.

I became excited after hearing some of Billy's experiences with FAITH presentations in which several people accepted Jesus as Savior. Billy told me to call Dr. Larry Williams at Broadmoor Baptist Church in Shreveport, which is where he had studied the evangelism strategy. As providence would have it, it turned out that the next course was starting in just two days.

The FAITH course was real work, but I had just retired from private practice and needed a challenge. The folks at Broadmoor turned out to be some of the nicest people you could ever meet. I usually filled in with a team that didn't have its full complement of three members. The third week I even filled in as "leader." During that night's visitation, our group stumbled through the presentation to a 16-year-old girl standing in her doorway. Our awkward presentation of the gospel didn't seem to bother her; she still accepted Jesus as Savior. I remember it as clear evidence of an important truth: all you have to do is *share*.

Training in evangelism is truly a marvelous experience, and that was certainly the case for me. Once I completed the course and had the knowledge of how to witness, my next step was to carry out that work.

I had one of my first chances in June of 2000. It was while I was in south Benin, Africa, on a medical mission trip with a group from Florida that I was able to put forward a form of the FAITH presentation. At least 36 people accepted Jesus as Savior after I presented the gospel to them.

Then, in late June and early July of that year I went to Cordoba, Mexico with the medical mission team from Broadmoor. Once we were there, I decided to go along with a group headed "out to the countryside." Dr. Stephen Patton, a

A FAITH training session.

nephrologist from Shreveport, led our team to southern Mexico, just a few miles north of Guatemala.

There I evaluated, diagnosed, and treated each person I saw. And after that I witnessed to each and every one of them. I used a presentation similar to FAITH and saw a few dozen people accept Jesus as Savior. Their names were recorded for local pastors who would follow up. One pastor said his church had more than doubled since the medical team had visited the year before.

I had agreed to go back to Rio de Janeiro to work with a returning team sponsored by the Tennessee Baptist Convention in mid 2002. Brenda Wisdom, R.N., was coordinating the trip and asked me to help with the medical team. Prior to departing for the trip to Rio, Brenda called and asked me to bring something she called an EvangeCube. She said that the missionary with whom we would be working had requested we bring one as they had been having great results using them.

On the airplane to Brazil I got out the EvangeCube and studied the instructions and Bible verses. During the week I shared the gospel via the EvangeCube (and an interpreter) to patients after I had diagnosed and treated them. The people were absolutely mesmerized by the powerful pictures and symbols on the cube, along with the gospel message that accompanied it. Simply put, I think the EvangeCube is the most effective evangelical tool I have ever utilized. In fact, that first week several dozen souls accepted Jesus as Savior as I used it, and the team as a whole saw several hundred people accept Jesus.

I now have taken the FAITH course four times and find it to be most useful in a Sunday school setting rather than a one-on-one conversation. For that situation, nothing seems to beat a simple presentation using the EvangeCube. For example, during five days of a medical clinic we conducted in North Benin during January 2005, our team of Rev. Stan Horton, missionary Lin Pinter, and my Beninese friend, Cyprien, witnessed 744 people accept Jesus as their Savior. In February of 2005 and 2006 in the Philippines, we counted 1,785 souls who came to a saving knowledge of Jesus as Savior through the EvangeCube.

(For more information on both the FAITH strategy and the EvangeCube, see the appendix at the end of this book.)

Chapter 4
Prayer

*Effective prayer is when you talk to God —
and then listen to what he says to you.*

Prayer is essential to any service we do for Jesus, especially any related to accomplishing the Great Commission. Prayer is where the power comes from.

This wasn't easy for me, however. Whenever it came time to pray in front of others, I used to cringe; I was afraid I would be called on. What would I say?

Finally, in January 2000 I got tired of feeling that way. I logged onto Amazon.com and looked up everything they had on prayer. Incredibly, there were about 4,500 items available, so I refined my search to *how* to pray. That time only 17 items popped up, two of which were titled exactly that: *How to Pray*. The first was by Ronnie W. Floyd and the second by R.A. Torrey. I ordered them both. R.A. Torrey (1856-1928) was an American evangelist, pastor, educator, and writer who taught at the Moody Bible Institute, and his was a very good book. But for me it was eclipsed by *How to Pray* by Dr. Ronnie W. Floyd, who is pastor of the First Baptist Church in Springdale, Arkansas. So enthused was I by his book that I bought several copies and gave them to my Sunday School class, pastor, associate pastor, and several others.

I also sent one to my friend Stan Horton, who also happened to be interested in prayer at that time. After he read it, he suggested I try to purchase Dr. Floyd's *How to Pray* in volume at wholesale cost. I ended up ordering 100 books. When I started distributing them, they went fast.

After another friend, William L. Bailey (or, as I call him, Bill Bailey 2) read his copy, he went so far as to volunteer to share the cost of another 100. We started giving out copies of *How to Pray* to new members as well as during church visitations. If you're interested in *How to Pray*, I'm all out of copies, but it is available online. I recommend it right next to the Holy Bible.

One of the things Dr. Floyd reminds us of in his *How to Pray* is exactly what prayer is. It is the means by which we can know God and his will for us. Prayer is how we talk with God. Through it we gain spiritual power. All of this is modeled by Jesus Christ, as in the Lord's Prayer (Matt. 5: 9-13). Prayer is the key that unlocks the door to God's throne room.

Prayer is not an option; it is essential. The last thing that your enemy, Satan, wants you to do is to learn how to pray effectively. And what makes a prayer effective? It's the kind that occurs when you talk to God and *then listen to what he is saying*. That is what prayer is all about. Prayer does not move God as much as it moves us toward God. When we pray, God is more likely to meet our needs. The greatest habit you can ever establish is to have a meaningful time with God daily.

My friend Stan, whose own absorption with prayer led him to suggest I buy *How to Pray* wholesale, was instrumental in my church establishing a dynamic prayer ministry. Today Stan is a minister of intercessory prayer, but for years I knew him from my medical practice when he was a drug representative for Dupont and made regular sales calls to my office. When he was called to be an intercessory prayer minister, I was honored to attend his ordination service in Coushatta, LA.

Rev. Stan Horton, the minister who helped start our prayer ministry at Airline Baptist Church. He also went to Benin, Africa on a medical missionary trip. He and two others helped lead 741 people to a saving knowledge of Jesus.

It was in mid-2000 when Stan called and told me about an amazing little book that I should read as soon as possible. I immediately ordered the book: *The Prayer of Jabez* by Bruce Wilkinson. The day after it arrived, I already had it read. I was so enthused about the book that I ordered 170 copies to give out during a presentation about my medical mission trip to Benin, Africa that I was scheduled to give at my church one Sunday night. That night almost no one had heard of or read the book. Later I had so many people tell me what a blessing the prayer had been to their life.

Dr. Vaughn was always amazed by the crowds that attended my presentations, but it was because I made of point of enticing people to attend. I always called a number of people who were, for instance, former patients or perhaps someone interested in missions, and then I offered to give them something like a book. I was glad for the chance to offer my audience something as wonderful as *The Prayer of Jabez*.

When Jabez's words from I Chronicles 4: 9-10 are prayed daily with sincerity, they become a powerful prayer:

"Oh, that you would bless me and enlarge my territory! Let your hand be with me, and keep me from harm so that I will be free from pain."

During a number of medical missions, I almost have to stop praying the Prayer of Jabez because God is exceedingly abundant beyond all expectations in answering prayers when you are doing his work. Asking that your territory be enlarged is exactly what he wants you to ask for, and he will bless you by answering.

Back to Stan and the church prayer ministry. He often gave me updates on the ministry he helped establish at his church. More and more people were joining in, making it very effective. He and I talked about beginning a similar prayer ministry at my church, and he agreed to come to Airline Baptist Church to talk to a small group I invited to serve as an initial core group.

Prayer warriors Vickie, Dan Adams, and Susan Hartsfield in the prayer room on a Sunday morning.

Eventually, in 2006, our church implemented a prayer ministry. Since then, our group has grown so much that we now have no problem staffing the prayer room throughout the day on Sunday. There is someone praying early Sunday morning before church starts from 7:00 to 7:45, then from 8 to 9 a.m. and 11 to 11:45 while worship services are going on. Eventually we hope to have a prayer room open 24 hours a day.

Meanwhile, prayer warriors in the prayer room petition God on behalf of our pastor, the services, our church, and a great many individual prayer requests. The list of things to pray for always includes our mission efforts, which — thanks to these warriors — are blessedly bathed in prayer.

Prayer committee members are not the only ones praying for our Great Commission efforts; we are also blessed to have praying for us my Sunday school class and department, my wife, and others — including Stan himself, who always keeps up with each of our mission trips so he can pray for me.

CHAPTER 5
Church Visitation

Church visitation has been labeled by many as the hardest job in town.

Visitation is the hardest job in town? Really? Yes, it certainly can be, unless it is organized and done properly.

On a Monday or Tuesday night for years I showed up for visitation, with the visitation group getting smaller and smaller week by week. Determined not to give in to discouragement, I kept going and kept trying. I told those I visited that we had a good church, a fine pastor, and a great Sunday school. Occasionally I would recognize that the person with whom I was talking really needed to hear the gospel and be told how to be saved, but I felt quite inadequate to make such a presentation. And the truth is that unless we are properly trained and organized, making that kind of presentation is almost always a futile exercise. First, you must have a group that is trained in evangelism and knows how to share Jesus and present salvation.

Experience has taught me that this is best accomplished with a program like FAITH where the pastor and staff are fully involved in the process, followed by the whole church body that gets involved either directly or indirectly.

Without a doubt, the FAITH method is the best program for Sunday school classes and churches. This requires that pastors and their staff take the responsibility for getting trained in Daytona Beach, Florida, or at some other church offering the program. This is a major commitment! It requires a major chunk of time: 16 weeks. It is no small thing to find people who are willing to give their time one evening per week for 16 weeks and who also have the enthusiasm to learn and share the text of the FAITH book. It requires ministerial visits each week for a chance to practice the FAITH version of the gospel, and followup visits are also a must. However, when done right, the result is absolutely awesome. Your church and Sunday school are certain to grow. When you go to the lost, the lost will come to you.

I won't, however, sugar coat the reality of visiting strangers to tell them about Jesus. Occasionally our group has had the door slammed in our faces. We have been told to leave . . . they are not interested . . . we are wasting their time. Once, after we had already been invited inside, we were told to leave. They didn't want to hear about our Jesus; they were of a different religion and didn't believe in him.

And yet all that pales in the face of the up side. The highlight of the FAITH course is, naturally, having someone pray the prayer of salvation to receive Jesus as Savior. This gets contagious as the group meets to share their results at the end of each visitation time. But such a presentation isn't limited to formal visitation efforts. Just as important is the everyday witness in which you offer the FAITH presentation as you go about your daily business.

A few years ago my wife, Vickie, and I were asked by members from our church to go visit a 92-year-old lady who was in the hospital and not doing well. According to the granddaughter, the lady had never accepted Jesus as Savior, and the family wanted us to witness to her. After praying for wisdom, discernment, and guidance, Vickie and I went to see the lady. She was very cordial and was amenable to listen to the FAITH presentation. Gently we offered her the gospel. You can imagine how elated we were when she said she would be delighted to accept Jesus into her heart. After a few more words and a prayer of thanksgiving, Vickie and I left to celebrate victory for Jesus. Less than two weeks later, this grand old lady went to be with her Savior.

On another occasion, a visitor to my Sunday school class asked me to visit a relative who was at Grace Home where terminally ill patients are treated. The visitor and his wife were unsure of her father's salvation.

I went with them to visit the dying father, and not long into our conversation I asked if I could show him something. I pulled out my EvangeCube and presented the plan of salvation. The relative assured me he had known Jesus for some time and was certain he was going to heaven. He did not live long; about two weeks later he quietly went to sleep and was off to spend eternity with Jesus. Because of the easy conversation using the EvangeCube, his daughter was gifted with the peace of knowing she would one day see her dad again.

The bottom line is that church visitation doesn't have to be the hardest job in town. If powered by prayer, proper organization, and training, visitation can be a highlight of your church experience.

CHAPTER 6

The Gideons

Wow!! What an organization.

From: Bill
Subject: Prison ministry tonight
Date: Oct. 4, 2007
To: Billy [Gideon and chair of Bible distribution]
    Mac [Gideon and chair of church relations]

Ron Hauser, Paul Vardeman, and I went to the maximum-security prison tonight and took 100 Gideon NKJV Bibles along. We gave out all 100. The people literally ran to get their own private copy. I gave out the Bibles in the conference room so I could talk with all those interested. I presented the gospel with the EvangeCube, and the inmates listened and watched with great interest. The Holy Spirit was there for sure. I asked if anyone was not sure of his salvation through Jesus Christ, and seven accepted Jesus for the first time. These men were very sincere and seemed to have a burden lifted from their shoulders. About half of the seven cried tears of joy.

Besides that, the prayer ministry in the prison is growing by leaps and bounds. Tonight I was given nine full pages — filled front and back — of prayer requests. We also had special prayer for a couple of the prisoners. One young man was crying because a relative had less than three hours to live after suffering a major stroke. Another inmate requested prayer because of some special family problems.

When we got back in the car to come home, we felt humbled by the events God had allowed us to participate in. We prayed again together, asking God to answer the nine pages of prayer requests according to his will.

The inmates asked once again if we could bring some Bible study guides; they want those almost as much as the Bible itself. Our pastor at Airline Baptist Church, Chad Grayson, is going to try to get a budget for the prison ministry so we can buy Bibles and Bible study materials for the men.

What a blessing we had tonight sharing the word of Jesus. Besides those who accepted Jesus tonight, we were blessed by how appreciative the prisoners were of us coming. The guards were extremely pleasant, helpful, and cooperative tonight.

It makes me proud to be a Gideon. God's Word will not return void. What a feeling to be able to share his Word and then see people pray to accept Jesus as their Lord and Savior.

It was a couple of years before I sent the victorious email above that Ron Hauser, a very faithful member of my Sunday school class, invited me to the Sunday morning prayer meeting of the local association of The Gideons International. At first I was a bit hesitant about going along with him, but after hearing Ron talk about the Gideons Sunday morning after Sunday morning, I decided to go.

I was pleasantly surprised at the meeting. I knew several of the men there, and I seemed to fit right in. The format and content of the prayer meeting were significant. I found out that their objective was the same as mine: winning others to Jesus Christ, or, in other words, the Great Commission. After going a couple of Sunday mornings, I decided to join.

One of the major objectives of The Gideons is to provide God's Word to people. The group in Bossier City frequently breaks into small groups to distribute Bibles and New Testaments to hotels, motels, nursing homes, schools (where allowed), and prisons. After joining The Gideons, I learned that there are more than 2 million new readers in the world every week, creating an unprecedented need for reading material. And there is no better material to read than the Holy Bible. Annually The Gideons International distributes more than 65 million copies of the Scriptures worldwide. This averages greater than 1 million copies of God's Word every 6 days, or 120 copies per minute. Wow!! What an organization.

Not long after joining The Gideons, I was invited to go to the Bossier Parish Minimum Security Prison. One Sunday, church member Dan Adams asked if anyone had a large-print Bible he could borrow for one of the prisoners he visited. I had one left over from a recent mission trip to the Philippines and was happy to offer it to him. We got to talking about the prison ministry, and Dan invited me to go along. After getting the necessary security clearance, recommendations from clergy, and an I.D. card at the sheriff's office, I was cleared for a visit. Before I went, though, I asked the Gideon chairman of distribution about getting some Scriptures to give out when I went. In fact, once I started participating in the prison ministry, I got a little embarrassed at how many Scriptures I was taking out of the Gideon storehouse. I tried once to apologize, but the reply I got from my fellow Gideon was, "That's what we are in the business of doing: giving out the Holy Bible to whoever needs it."

Being a Gideon representative in the prison system is an honor; I am always happy to write *Gideon, Bossier Camp* by my name when I go on visitation. As the Bossier Gideons' contact for visitation to the Bossier Parish Prison, I try to help them make sure that all prisoners who want one have a Holy Bible. Our group has handed out hundreds of Scriptures, and we personally witness to every prisoner who will listen. In the last

A Saturday morning prayer meeting with The Gideons.

two years, more than 300 men have come to a saving knowledge of Jesus Christ, and we are all excited about going again almost every week. I'll tell you more about the prison ministry in a later chapter.

Being a Gideon has led to other opportunities as well. Several times I've given talks to other Gideons about personal witnessing. The first was at the west Shreveport Gideon meeting. Afterward, a member of the group, Dr. Ben Singletary, told me my talk made him proud to be a doctor. It was one of the best compliments I have ever received. On the heels of that talk, I was asked to speak to the Bossier City Gideon group, and then at Bellaire Baptist Church. A lady at one of the presentations emailed me about going on an international medical mission trip with our group. Subsequently, she went with us on our Ukraine medical mission trip.

If you're interested, The Gideons actively recruit qualified members. More information can be found at www.gideons.org, or you can contact your local Gideons.

CHAPTER 7

Prison Ministry

*When I ask a new believer, "Where does Jesus live now?"
the answer I love to hear is: "He lives in my heart."*

The very first time I visited the prison, I quickly understood just how much the inmates lost when they lost their freedom. After I walked through that big metal door and heard it shut with a hollow bang, the reality of the prisoners' plight hit me hard.

The prisons are divided into dorms, also called pods, and we enter each one through two doors that have to be electronically opened for us to enter. At first I wasn't sure what to expect of the inmates, but I quickly learned that the prisoners were *happy to see us.*

When I told them I had Gideon Bibles to give them, we got swarmed; almost everyone wanted a Bible of his own. It wasn't long before the prisoners *ran* to get a Bible. We didn't always have enough to go around, and they soon learned to sprint if they wanted a copy of God's Word. During these first visits, it wasn't unusual to have as many as 18 inmates accept Jesus as Savior each time we went.

There was one night at the minimum-security prison that the three of us in the prison ministry team felt an uncomfortable kinship to the Three Hebrew Children as they neared the fiery furnace. It seems one of the prisoners had set off the fire alarm, causing all the vents to every dorm to close automatically. Remember, this was Louisiana. The temperature outside was 95 degrees that evening — hot enough that the prisoners, in an effort to keep cool, were taking more frequent showers. Maybe it wasn't quite a furnace, but the combination of stifling heat, natural Louisiana humidity, moisture from the showers, and the closed vents, had turned the prison into a hot, muggy mess. Condensation on the floor made walking a hazard. We almost had to struggle to breathe.

Despite conditions that would have made some saints irritable and short-tempered — much less a bunch of convicts — we had a wonderful visit with the men. When they saw that we had the much-sought-after Gideon Bibles, they rushed us. I confess that it was nice to run out of Bibles so fast because it allowed me to return to the air-conditioned security office for more copies — not once, but twice.

At the end of our visit that night, Dan Adams' shirt did not have a dry thread on it. Twice Ron Hauser was forced to retreat to the security office to cool off he was so hot. In spite of all that, the Holy Spirit was very much in attendance that night. All three of us had the honor of leading men to salvation.

Ron Hauser and I reported to my Sunday school class on a regular basis about the prison ministry; the people in the class enjoyed hearing about the fantastic results we were having. It wasn't long before a couple more men got their credentials and clearance, enabling us to send three or four men to the minimum-security prison on almost a weekly basis. Like Jabez, we too wanted to expand our borders, so we sought and received permission to expand our prison ministry to include the medium and even maximum-security prisons just up the road.

Before I got too busy at these local facilities, I was also able to visit a prison in another parish: Wade Correctional Institute in Caddo Parish. One Saturday there I had 18 accept Jesus. It was interesting: the more we went to Wade Correctional Institute, the more disturbed the followers of Islam became. On more than one occasion, one fellow would get his blanket or cardboard and go to a corner, face eastward, and start praying to Allah. At other times he might listen to the message, but his face would turn into an impenetrable stone wall. But on at least two occasions, prisoners who were studying to be a Muslim came, listened to the message, heard the gospel via the EvangeCube, and then accepted Jesus as their Savior.

Afterward, I made a point of reminding them that God is a jealous God and does not tolerate having other religions before him, and they agreed.

One night at the minimum-security prison, I was using the EvangeCube to deliver the salvation message to a group of about 10 when a Muslim inmate interrupted.

"There is only one god," he said, "and it is Allah."

Before I could say anything, one of the black prisoners spoke up. "Hush!" he said. "Listen to the man. He's trying to tell you about the love of Jesus."

As if that weren't good enough, all the other inmates there chimed in, admonishing the Muslim inmate to listen.

Man, that made my week! Their surprisingly sweet attitude and genuine respect for the Lord are part of what make the trips to the prison so worthwhile. Time and again we've seen how willing the prisoners are to learn about God. On several occasions I have told them the story of Gideon from the Book of Judges and reminded them that the Bible is a treasure of real stories just like that. But whatever sermon or lesson we bring, they have proven they love to listen to any message from the Bible.

Sometimes we take our Sunday school classes' out-of-date Explore the Bible commentaries to offer to those prisoners who want to study the Bible in-depth. That is the request we hear more and more from the men: They want more materials to help them study God's Word. Eventually I wrote LifeWay Stores in Nashville and requested their surplus materials, and they graciously consented to send some. I also asked for "Open Windows," a booklet that combines daily Scripture reading with devotions, and another devotion book, "Daily Bread." LifeWay was good enough to send a large boxful.

It turned out the prisoners swarmed me even more for those books than they did the Bibles, because by then we had handed out so many Scriptures that we had finally met the largest demand. Now everyone wants to learn more about their Bible, and we run out of study materials quickly. But how encouraging it is to see men so hungry to know God better! And they're still asking for more, so we have asked all our adult Sunday school classes to save their quarterly Bible study guides so we can pass them along to the prisoners.

I remember the first time our group went to the new maximum-security prison. We were never made to feel any more welcome in our lives than we were that night. But I didn't yet have that assurance when the guard escorted us to the room where we would be speaking. He strode into the room full of inmates and snapped off the TV. I think we all were a bit intimidated as the officer barked to the men to either listen to this minister or go to the back of the room. But we needn't have worried. I have rarely been as well received as a friend as I was that night. The maximum-security prisoners were much like their brethren in the minimum-security facility: happy to receive the Gideon Bibles and glad to listen to a message of Jesus' love for them. Many accepted him as their Savior.

If you're looking for an environment where you can grow into a Great Commission Christian, I highly recommend participating in a prison ministry. It's a setting where you can learn what your particular God-given gift is. Or, if you already know, where you can mature your gift while being a blessing to a good many captive souls.

Take our group, for instance. Dan Adams is more of a teacher; he loves to get a group of 12 to 15 people lined up at a table or in the conference room and give them a "Sunday school lesson" or study a particular idea in the Bible. At the end of the session, he always asks if anyone would like to accept Jesus as Savior. Frequently many do.

Ron Hauser and I deliver a batch of new Gideon Bibles to the medium-security facility in Bossier Parish.

Glen Carter, on the other hand, loves to get one-on-one and use the EvangeCube to present the gospel. He has led many to Christ doing so.

Ron Hauser loves the prison ministry; he is always raring to go on prison nights. He had set a personal goal of guiding 72 people to Jesus by the time he was 72. Well, he has already reached that goal and is still going strong.

Paul Vardeman, who had experience with a prison ministry before joining our group, prefers a mixture of teaching and evangelism and does well on the visitation presenting the Word.

Personally, I enjoy using the EvangeCube. That "magic cube" just seems to fascinate people. But while taking the FAITH course for the fourth time, I found that making the presentation to prisoners was excellent practice and that they were just as responsive to that form of the gospel. Several inmates accepted Jesus as their Savior after they heard the FAITH message.

Several times I've had to part with my beloved EvangeCube, however. Whenever a prisoner has asked for it so that he might share the gospel with his fellow cellmates, I haven't had the heart to say no. After all, I can certainly understand their desire to be a Great Commission Christian — and there's no better place to be one than in a prison where the gospel is so desperately needed.

In the last two years, our prison ministry group has seen well more than 300 men accept Jesus as Savior. Afterward, I often remark to the new Christian that he may have been brought to prison for a reason: so he could find Jesus as Savior. I also ask, "Where does Jesus live now?" I almost always get the jubilant answer: "He lives in my heart!"

CHAPTER 8

Mission Trips Abroad

The fields of harvest are many;
the missionaries await the workers.

My first 30 medical mission trips abroad were chronicled in an earlier book, *You Will Never Run Out of Jesus*. Since then I have continued to go abroad on mission trips, some of which I coordinate and others in which I participate as a team member.

A mission trip abroad is only one method of being a Great Commission Christian, but it has been one of my favorites. I have been to Central and South America, Asia, Eastern Europe, the Pacific area, and several countries in Africa. Wherever I go, there are always people who really need to hear the good news of Jesus.

The first few of out-of-country mission trips I made were a result of my personal contact with members of my local medical community in Louisiana. These trips began in 1999, the year following my baptism in the Jordan River to consecrate myself to spreading the gospel.

Then, soon after I retired from private practice in order to devote myself to becoming a Great Commission Christian, I was put in contact with a wonderful group, the Baptist Medical and Dental Fellowship, which expanded my overseas mission opportunities.

A member of the BMDF board who had spoken at my church directed me to BMDF headquarters to find out what mission opportunities were available. That eventually led to my contacting a missionary in Thailand. A group from my church and I joined another group from Florida and headed to Southeast Asia where we conducted a mobile clinic in which we pulled teeth, treated goiters, and more.

My relationship with BMDF was cemented, as it was with the Florida group, with whom I have since made three other overseas mission trips.

After a solid induction into international medical missions trips, I soon found it easy to obtain information about going to all parts of the globe. Along the way, another thing I had learned was how much work it is to coordinate such a trip. The logistics are formidable.

First and foremost is selecting a place to go and receiving an invitation from either the missionary working there or from the group sponsoring mission work in that location. Invitations are not hard to come by; missionaries have found that bringing in short-term volunteer medical groups to proffer physical and spiritual aid is one of the very best ways to minister to the people. It also helps build churches because medical groups attract crowds to the clinic site. All in all, medical missions support missionaries' ultimate goal: spreading the gospel of Jesus.

After determining a destination, we communicate further with the missionary or group stationed there to learn what our primary medical focus should be. We have found the best approach is to just turn ourselves over to the missionary for guidance. Sometimes the trip is strictly surgical. In Guatemala, for instance, we often work in a hospital doing general surgery, or obstetrical/gynecological surgery if we have brought ob-gyn doctors along.

At other times, such as during a recent trip to Ghana, we conduct medical and surgical clinics as well as emergency surgeries when needed. When the need arises (and that is fairly often), I pull teeth. I may conduct minor surgery out in the field or just offer an on-the-spot medical clinic when the people need one. Such clinics are what most missionaries ask for when we contact them about making a visit. And whether we conduct the clinic in churches, schools, or under a mango tree, the objective is the same: to attract people, show them the love of Jesus, and offer them the gospel message.

Almost always, we are faced with more people who need treatment than any of us can get to, but we do the best we can.

In our initial discussion with missionaries, we also get their input on how many volunteers should constitute the team for that particular trip. Frequently we are limited by the availability of transportation and sleeping quarters. Sometimes we are forced to take a smaller team because of how many interpreters the missionary is able to provide. Within the month I'll be taking a group to Kampong Cham, Cambodia, for a medical and dental clinic, and the missionary there has requested a team of 12 to 15, the limiting factor being the supply of good English interpreters.

Once we know what our medical focus will be and how many volunteers we should take, it's then time to recruit the team. I usually try to recruit an extra person or two because it seems someone always has to drop out.

And, of course, there is always the matter of money. Each team member is responsible for his or her own expenses. The missionary at our destination provides an estimate of what the in-country expenses will be. Usually these are very sound as the missionary is aware of the most reasonable places to stay and eat — and even the best places to go for some R & R. Following the missionaries' advice has always been the best formula. When it comes to air travel, we work through a mission-oriented travel agency to get the most reliable, affordable rates.

I work as an ER doctor to fund my trips, but occasionally I receive a donation. For instance, one time when I was working in an ER in Mansfield, LA, a woman who had read an article about my mission trips came to talk with me. Her church ultimately donated more than $3,000 to my group. That paid for more than half of a mission trip!

Securing the many medical and dental supplies needed for each trip is a vital part of trip logistics, and these I have obtained from several sources. The hospitals where I've worked as an emergency room physician have been good to donate large amounts of surgical instruments and soon-to-expire medical supplies. They also have always been willing to autoclave, or sterilize, instruments for me. Other sources — and some of the best — are Alcon Laboratories and Kingsway Charities, which very graciously provide the supplies for free. Other reliable resources offering very reasonable prices are Blessings International, CrossLink International, MAP International, World Dental Relief, and several others. I am sure many others have their favorites as well.

Transporting all the supplies is the next demanding step. Frequently the missionary is required to furnish a manifest as

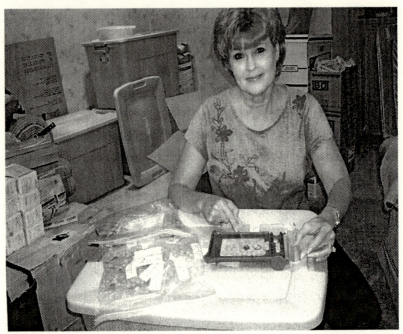

Vickie Bailey counts medicine in preparation for a trip to Cambodia in 2007.

part of getting our supplies cleared with the Minister of Health in that country. This requires a detailed inventory of everything from medicines and suture materials to surgical and dental instruments, including each item's name, quantity, manufacturer, serial number, and expiration date. Some countries even require that the retail value be listed. I'm lucky that my wife, Vickie, does most of this for me. Then comes the packing; I take most of the supplies in a second suitcase or trunk, although some missionaries advise against using trunks as this brings attention to the supplies, causing them to be closely scrutinized by custom officials — a time-consuming process. Another hitch is that the airlines sometimes lose the supplies, delaying or even preventing their arrival in the field. When that happens, we have to buy everything in-country, and that can be a real problem, especially within our limited budget.

The logistics of making a medical mission trip abroad is often made even more interesting with in-country travel arrangements. Usually this is organized by the missionary. Traveling to the work site can sometimes be time-consuming — and occasionally downright hazardous. I once was in an accident in which our vehicle flipped three times. In another country one of our vehicles ran into the back of the one ahead. Fortunately no one was hurt very badly in either incident.

Depending on where we conduct our work, lodging can pose another challenge. Usually the local missionary finds a nice, convenient place for our accommodations, but on one occasion we camped out in a school building, where, even though we were indoors, we still had to sleep inside tents in order to avoid the vicious mosquitoes. Another time part of my group was stuck in the middle of nowhere; they slept on cots draped in mosquito nets inside mud houses.

Beyond planning for supplies, travel, and lodging, however, is the most important planning of all — planning to present the gospel. Frequently this is coordinated with the missionary or a church group in the country. After seeing one used effectively in Kenya in 1999, I always like to have a spiritual station on the work site where the gospel can be presented. This is usually the last among the other clinic stations, which include:
- ♦ a large waiting area with an informal sentry (usually the missionary) posted at the entrance to the clinic to provide crucial crowd control;
- ♦ a triage station where patients needs are evaluated and then sent to one the following:
  - ♦ dental station,
  - ♦ medical station, or
  - ♦ nutrition care station;
- ♦ the pharmacy, which is frequently run by a certified

pharmacist, and is where patients can get free medicine and/or supplies; and
♦ the spiritual station.

Patients are asked to go to the spiritual station after they have been cared for physically. The station is usually little more than a table and a couple of chairs set up away from the hustle and bustle of the other treatment stations. Often it is staffed with a minister or someone else trained in presenting the plan of salvation. Here witnessing is done quietly and usually one-on-one, oftentimes using the EvangeCube or some other straightforward method of presenting the gospel. There are variations, depending on where we are ministering. In Cambodia, for instance, we use what the missionary calls "the religious towel." It's a large cloth with about 16 pictures — from the creation and the story of Abraham, to Jesus and his life, death, and resurrection. In this presentation, Abraham is emphasized because he is a spiritual figure to whom Muslims relate well. The spiritual station is the last one because we don't want patients to think they have to go there in order to be treated. We want to emphasize that our ministry is *free*; our treatment and

This is me packing supplies and medicine for a 2007 medical mission trip.

medications are theirs at no charge. It is especially important that they understand the spiritual instruction is something we also offer freely ... to be accepted freely — or not. The spiritual station is the most important station in the clinic. What happens there is really what we are there for.

Those who respond to the gospel message are recorded and given to the missionary or church for followup. It happens that the missionary in Cambodia has said he sometimes finds that when he returns to the villages to follow up with those who had said they had surrendered to Jesus, he learns that they had not truly done so.

As a result, what we are now doing at the spiritual station there is praying with the people only *about* salvation, asking them to seriously consider surrrendering their lives to Christ. It is important that we follow the missionaries' lead in such matters. While it may be my calling to focus on the first part of the Great Commission, I know that the hardest part is the second: To teach them whatsoever I have commanded you. This is the part the missionary must see to after we leave.

If planning to present the gospel is one of the more demanding elements of preparation, then recruiting team members to make that possible is sometimes the most enjoyable. However, the fact that it's gratifying to offer others the opportunity to share the Good News doesn't mean it's always easy. Finding nurses, nurse practitioners, doctors, and dentists who can break away to go at a specific time can be a chore. One strategy that helps is publicizing a trip on the BMDF or International Mission Board websites. One trip I organized included people from seven different states, which can be a challenge when it comes to coordinating the preparations. But it is amazing how the Lord can use so many different people to accomplish his tasks.

My continuing work as an emergency room physician not only helps fund my mission travels; it also provides great recruiting opportunities. I find another pool of recruits at my church; from the start I made a point of inviting my fellow congregants. When we first went to Cambodia I invited a number of people and six accepted, but after I returned and people learned what a great trip we had, many others wanted to go. Luckily, on the second trip to Cambodia, the missionaries had told us we could bring a bigger group, and I took 19 with us. The next year, 30 from my church wanted to go. I had to turn more than half of them down, as the missionaries had determined that, because of transportation issues and the number of interpreters available, they could accommodate only a dozen volunteers.

At any rate, my church family has come to know quite well how much I enjoy sharing the opportunity to be a Great Commission Christian. As one of the members of my Sunday school class says, "You can't come and expect to just listen to Dr. Bailey teach. When it comes to missions, he expects you to participate!"

In fact, I consider it one of the greatest accomplishments of my life that I am now commonly greeted with: "Dr. Bailey, where are you going next?"

CHAPTER 9

Personal Witnessing in the Work Place

Believers who are available to God become more sensitive and usable for spontaneous situations in which to share the gospel.

Building Bridges Through FAITH
(The Journey Continues)

Earlier in life, I often thought about witnessing to someone in my work place about Jesus Christ; however, a fear of how to do so properly — as well as a fear of what the consequences might be, including getting reprimanded — was always a deterrent. This was no phantom fear. Once while I was still in private practice a young man was specifically referred to me so that I might have the chance to pray for and witness to him. When I recommended to the young man that he get down on his knees and pray regularly, he got upset and later reported me to the local medical society.

Despite my fears and that unhappy experience, I did eventually become more comfortable witnessing, largely because of my church visitation and mission experience. Such practice — not to mention seeing the results of the Holy Spirit drawing sinners to accept Christ — is the best way to discover and get comfortable with your personal witnessing style.

I believe many of the most important witnessing opportunities we'll ever have are ordinary, everyday workday situations that we just need to recognize and take advantage of. One such opportunity arose in an emergency room where I often work. I was presented with a young person dependent on prescription medications; he was called a "frequent flyer" by the ER staff because he repeatedly came in with all kinds of complaints in hopes of getting narcotics of some type. After talking with him in the presence of his mother, I told him he needed a purpose in life and a major change in direction. I asked to be excused for a moment and hurried out to my car where I keep an EvangeCube for just such moments. Back inside, I proceeded to carefully explain the love of God and his need for accepting that love and for giving his life over to Jesus. After a slightly emotional moment and a few tears, the young man received Jesus as his Lord and Master. His mother was delighted, and both seemed to have received a blessing of peace that one can hardly imagine. I told him and his mother that he now needed to confirm and seal the moment by going to their church and making his decision public; both agreed. No prescription of meds was necessary. A little touch of heaven left with them that day.

Divine appointments do happen. While I usually refuse to work on Sundays in order to teach my Sunday school class and attend all the church services, perhaps it was God's timing that one Sunday as I was working in an ER I was presented a young woman, a sophomore in college, who had attempted suicide by overdosing on some over-the-counter medications. I listened to her sad story. She had few friends, no goal in life, and a recent tangle of missteps. After doing a physical and completing the required lab work, I consulted social services about possible placement for her in a facility if needed. The social worker set up an outpatient appointment for counseling and had the young lady sign it. But I sensed an immediate need for her to find the right direction and a real purpose in her life, so I excused myself briefly and went to get my EvangeCube. I returned to her bedside, and right there, in the presence of her aunt, I presented the gospel story and emphasized her need for the loving care of the Savior. She accepted Jesus, and immediately, peace, comfort, and reassurance were evident upon her face. Her aunt was so pleased. After an admonition to go to church and make her decision public and to follow up with regular church attendance, I left the two of them in a much healthier frame of mind.

Soon another opportunity arose. It was early one morning in the ER when a young mother came in. She was from distant state and had come to town to escape the wrath of her abusive husband. She had run away once before, she explained, but her husband had discovered her whereabouts and had beaten her into submission once again. When finally she could stand it no longer, she sought the solace of a friend who had helped her find her way to our city and, hopefully, a new life.

As I listened and saw the tears produced by a torn and abusive relationship, I sensed a much deeper need than the simple physical matter that had brought her into the hospital. I asked about her spiritual life. She hadn't had one for some time, she said. I asked if she would allow me to share with her and her friend about the love of Jesus. She agreed, so I quickly went to get my EvangeCube and presented the salvation story to her and her friend. She agreed right then and there to pray to receive

Jesus as the Lord of her life. When I explained that she needed to make her decision public in a church, her friend promised that she could help with that part. A glow of contentment and peace appeared on the young mother's face that I will not soon forget.

At another hospital, a particularly bright student working to become a physician assistant recently arrived for her rotation through the emergency room. The two of us happened to get into a discussion about religion, and I detected that she was not a committed Christian. I shared with her that I made frequent medical mission trips to foreign lands and gave her a copy of my book, *You Will Never Run Out of Jesus*.

In the next four weeks I did what I could to win her confidence. Then, on the last day we were scheduled to work together, I asked the student for a conference. Together we went to the hospital lounge, and I showed her the EvangeCube, explaining that I used it to tell others the gospel. When I asked if she was a Christian, she said she thought so, but when I asked if she would go to heaven if she died right now, she said she wasn't sure.

I presented the gospel using the EvangeCube, and she then prayed to have Jesus come into her heart. I instructed her to read the Gospel of John followed by Ephesians Chapter 1 to assure her of her salvation. She agreed and seemed very happy.

Perhaps a divine appointment awaits you, too. As they teach us in FAITH training, "Believers who are available to God become more sensitive and usable for spontaneous situations in which to minister or share the gospel." God will let you know what to say and do at the appointed time. Remember Jesus' words:

> "[D]o not worry about what to say or how to say it. At that time you will be given what to say, for

it will not be you speaking, but the Spirit of your Father speaking through you."

Matthew 10:19-20, New International Version

CHAPTER 10

Sharing Jesus Without Fear

*"So shall my word that goeth out my mouth;
it shall not return unto me void, but it shall accomplish
that which I please, and it shall prosper in the thing
whereto I sent it."*

Isaiah 55:11

Don't be one of those who talks about *the lost.
Be one who talks* to *the lost.*

Success is sharing your faith and living for Jesus Christ, and with a promise like the one in Isaiah above, you cannot fail.

Success has nothing whatsoever to do with whether you win anyone to the Lord. You cannot save anyone. Results are not always immediate, but obedience should be. And when you share, you are being obedient. Better to be one who talks *to* the lost than *about* them.

The Great Commission instructs: God has called each of us to share our faith. If you will simply go, God will enable you with the Holy Spirit.

Someone once asked if God was so great, could he build a wall so strong that even he could not break it down. The next question, of course, was meant to be something of a brainteaser: If God is so great, then why couldn't he break the wall down?

Well, God has already created a wall like that; it is called the human heart. God is mighty enough, but he will never break through that wall. He will enter only if invited. That is where we come in. God wants to use each of us as a witness to present the gospel, which in turn can melt that heart to accept Jesus as Lord and Savior. Your chance is coming to use his words of truth as life preservers to rescue those drowning in the depths of their sin.

Jesus had no fear when he left all his teachings in the keeping of his disciples. He had confidence that the Holy Spirit would help the disciples take the gospel to the uttermost parts of the world. You too should have no fear. The Holy Spirit will guide you each time you share the gospel.

CHAPTER 11

Spiritual Warfare

Spiritual warfare exists in the unseen supernatural dimension, where God is all-powerful and Satan is in revolt.

AllAboutFollowingJesus.org

As the above quote from a website for All About God Ministries suggests, spiritual warfare is a very deep subject. So why do I include it in a chapter of a book that revolves around the Great Commission? Because spiritual warfare is real and affects our ability to witness!

In Ephesians, Paul speaks of the spiritual threats we face: "For we wrestle not against flesh and blood, but against principalities, against powers, against the rulers of the darkness of this world, against spiritual wickedness in high places" (Eph. 6:12). Paul then tells us in the next verse: "Wherefore take unto you the whole armour of God, that ye may be able to withstand in the evil day, having done all, to stand" (Eph. 6:13).

What we do for God bothers Satan to such an extent that he battles us in all aspects of our lives, especially when we are trying to accomplish the Great Commission and take someone to heaven with us.

The passages in Ephesians 6 tell us to buckle on the belt of truth, put on the breastplate of righteousness, strap on our sandals of peace, pick up our shield of faith, put on our helmet of salvation, and put the Sword of the Spirit on the tip of our tongues. Were it not for God's armor, I would have been a spiritual sitting duck on many a mission trip. On just about every international trip I have made, we have encountered some form of spiritual warfare. I'll share a few of these and their outcome with you.

In April of 2004 I went with a group of medical students from Louisiana State University on a trip to Honduras sponsored through Xtreme Team Mission Adventures. The trip had been quite productive. On the last day we got up at 3:45 a.m. to pack our suitcases in the three vehicles and then headed back to the airport at La Ceiba for the first leg of our journey home. As we were driving along, our driver, Marlin, bent over to pick up a cassette music tape off the floor. While doing so he lost control of our vehicle, and we hurtled off the highway going 55 mph.

Our vehicle tumbled down a hillside over and over. We rolled three times and landed on the vehicle's side. I had been in the backseat trying to sleep and did not have my seatbelt on. I was thrown about in the truck like a rag doll. This sure felt like spiritual warfare to me. Any or all of us could have been killed, but fortunately no one was significantly hurt. After we all crawled out of the vehicle, we held hands and prayed, thanking God for delivering us from almost certain injury. No doubt the Lord had his protective arms around us.

(You may be interested to know that Marlin later married one of the women on that trip. They now serve as missionaries, exploring the surrounding countryside identifying pockets of believers who would like to start a church.)

There is always a problem of one sort or another on mission trips. Big or small, we just have to pray and carry on.

On Feb. 20, 2006, a very unusual event took place in Bossier City and Shreveport. We had an ice storm, and all four bridges between Bossier City and Shreveport were closed because of the weather. That meant we had to delay our medical mission trip to the Philippines for at least one day. I cancelled all our flights and had to spend the next seven hours rescheduling. In the end, everything turned out fine. We all met in Detroit by the following evening and proceeded to the Philippines, where we enjoyed a very successful trip. Our spiritual team with Rev. Scotty Teague and Rev. Harrell Shelton saw 1,071 people pray to receive Jesus as their Savior. What a blessing; glory to God for overcoming the obstacles.

Another memorable trip was one we made to north Benin where IMB missionaries John and Suzanne Crocker were stationed. I had Stan Horton and Cyprien working in the spiritual station all week, and they did a fantastic job; 744 people accepted Jesus as Savior. On the way back from Natitingou to Cotonou, the driver of our lead vehicle had to slam on her brakes because a huge tanker truck was broken down in front of us. The second vehicle immediately behind crashed loudly into the rear of the first, sending glass flying everywhere. I was in the third vehicle, and when I saw what happened, I thought the second vehicle had hit a person. A mass of strangers had gathered along the roadside, and their murmurs filled us with a sense of evil. Talk about a tense atmosphere. No one had been hurt, but if one of the people there had been, we knew we would have been mobbed. It was inexplicable, but real: a true sense of spiritual warfare had struck. Ultimately the whole situation was defused by Cyprien; he had grown up in the area, and everyone related well to him. Thank God for answered prayers in those tense moments.

It was a few months later that real tragedy seemed to strike. The Crockers were met with a family situation that forced them to return home to Alabama. That left only three married missionary couples along with a few other missionaries in the whole country of Benin. I know they must have felt defeated by that particular spiritual war.

But sometimes it is the darkest just before the dawn. John is now head of missions at Whitesburg Baptist Church in Huntsville, Alabama. He goes on four to six international mission trips a year, taking his evangelistic teams and occasionally a medical team, and he has assured me that he is definitely reaching more people now.

Church visitation too does not go without its fair share of spiritual warfare. During my initial FAITH training at Broadmoor Baptist Church, it began to pour rain on the night we were supposed to make visitations. Earlier we had specifically prayed that the Lord would be honored during visitation that night, and so, not to be deterred, one group headed for an indoor mall. However, they had the chance to witness to only a few people before the mall manager asked them to leave. It seems someone had complained about being bothered by a religious group.

Rain was still coming down so hard that we couldn't walk door to door without getting soaked, and so our group made its way to a local laundromat. There we witnessed a number of people, all of whom were very receptive. Because we had not given up in the face of spiritual opposition, the trip was a fruitful one.

CHAPTER 12

Is Heaven Real?

Yes, I believe in heaven.

Heaven has been taught and preached to me since I can remember. While many have struggled to describe it, we know this: heaven represents the glorious eternal life that we will share with Jesus.

In John, Jesus says: "I have come that they may have life, and that they may have it more abundantly" (John 10:10, NKJV). Jesus is saying that after we accept him as Lord and Savior, the heaven we experience here on Earth is an abundant life. Later in the same chapter Jesus says, "And if I go and prepare a place for you, I will come again and receive you to Myself, that where I am, there you may be also" (John 14:3, NKJV). This is what we usually think of as heaven in the hereafter.

Heaven is best portrayed by John in the Book of Revelation, and he describes it as a magnificent place indeed. From Genesis to Revelation, the whole Bible points to heaven. I am trusting my everything on heaven being real. When I do personal witnessing or evangelism with the EvangeCube, I quote John 14:6 in which Jesus says, "I am the way, the truth, and the life; no man cometh unto the Father, but through me." I tell everyone that there is only one ticket to heaven ... and that ticket is found in that verse. You must believe in the Lord Jesus Christ.

I've had one close physical encounter with heaven. It happened when I almost drowned at age 9. My family was on the Sabine River (now Toledo Bend Lake) with one of my dad's friends, and the adults were gathering catalpa worms on the riverbank so they could go fishing that night. My two sisters, my brother, and I wandered about 200 yards farther down. We had been admonished *not* to go into the water until the adults could come to watch us, but, as adventurous children sometimes do, my sister and I started to wade into the water.

The previous year we had waded all the way across the river, and the water had never climbed above our waists. On that day, however, my sister Linda was suddenly swept away by the current. I made a reach for her, only to find myself in over my own head. This was bad. Not only was the current strong, but I also had never learned to swim. After a couple of minutes submerged beneath the water, I apparently went into a semi-conscious state. I saw the most exquisitely clear blue sky I had ever seen, and I experienced a complete silence that was the most peaceful and serene I had ever known.

Meanwhile, my 5-year-old brother Tommy had the presence of mind to go get my parents and my father's friend, Lee Whitlock. The next thing I remember was my dad using resuscitation measures on me after pulling me from the water. Lee swam out and retrieved Linda, who had been swept downstream but had not gone under.

Others have had even more intense encounters in the afterlife. Rev. Don Piper was run over by an 18-wheeler in January 1989 and was pronounced dead by paramedics. In his book, *90 Minutes in Heaven: A True Story of Death and Life*, he gives a very vivid description of what heaven is really like because *he was there!* The sights, colors, and sounds were beyond what words can adequately express. Don describes heaven as perfection. In his second book, *Heaven is Real: Lessons on Earthly Joy from the Man Who Spent 90 Minutes in Heaven*, Don says that the heavenly journey gave him a powerful assurance that heaven is real and a renewed confidence in the promises contained in the Bible.

For yet another account of "going to the other side," read about Rev. Frank E. Crawford's experience in the Appendix.

I've always believed in heaven because I trust God and his Word. But after reading Don Piper's books, I am even more motivated to give the good news of Jesus to as many as who will hear it so that they too may experience the reality of heaven.

CHAPTER 13
Drinking from my Saucer

*I'm drinking from my saucer,
because my cup has overflowed.*

John Paul Moore

T he greatest joy in life comes from obedience to the Lord. As you have no doubt gathered as you read through this book, I have learned the best way to be happy is, as hymn writer John Sammis penned more than a hundred years ago, to trust and obey, for there is no other way to be happy in Jesus. In fact, I also agree with another writer, John Paul Moore, when he said, "I am drinking from my saucer, because my cup has overflowed."

I am truly enjoying the second half of my life, the period following halftime. After realizing there had to be more to life than just being successful, I sought significance through my dream of fulfilling the Great Commission. Since retiring from private practice, I have begun to live that dream. I may not have accumulated a lot of riches after working for almost 40 years, but I have found work that occupies my time and carries results that will last for all eternity. I am drinking from my saucer, because my cup has overflowed.

Spiritual enemies have always been present, and the need to do spiritual warfare persists, but the Lord has given me strength and courage even when the way grows steep and rough. He has blessed me sufficiently. Indeed I am drinking from my saucer, because my cup has overflowed.

Joy is the product of our endeavors to commit to God's grand job for us: participating in the Great Commission. Joy still floods my heart as I think of all those I've known who have prayed the sinner's prayer and received Jesus as their Savior. To God goes the glory; I just want to praise him for the ways he has used me to fulfill the Great Commission. That reward is to walk the celestial streets of gold. I am drinking from my saucer, because my cup has overflowed.

Thanks to Jesus for loving me so much that he shed his blood on the cross, so that by his grace I have his salvation. I now will have eternal life and heaven. I am drinking from my saucer, because my cup has overflowed.

I am assured of my salvation as verified in Ephesians 1:13-14. And because of what Christ did, all you who have heard the Good News and have trusted Christ have been marked as belonging to Christ by the Holy Spirit, who long ago was promised to all of us Christians. His presence within us is God's guarantee that he has already purchased us and that he guarantees to bring us to himself. I am drinking from my saucer, because my cup has overflowed.

Yes, there is something better than going to heaven ... and that is taking someone with you.

APPENDIX

This section of the book contains EvangeCube visuals and information about the FAITH program. These are copyrighted materials frequently used by a host of organizations and churches. It also includes a final anecdote, "What's Important to You?" about one thing that truly matters in life.

Also below you will find the entire text of the email received from Rev. Frank E. Crawford of New Hebron, Mississippi.

Subject: DROWNING IN THE OCOEE RIVER
Date of email: 9/16/2007
From: Rev. Frank Crawford
To: Dr. Bill Bailey

Don Inman and I departed from Canton, NC about 10:00 a.m. Two gracious ladies had prepared us a picnic lunch to be eaten en route to Chattanooga, TN. Four hours into our trip, at 2:30 p.m., we stopped at a roadside park on the bank of the Ocoee River in east Tennessee. We knew that we were on a bank of a river, but there was no water in the river; all we could see was a beautiful rock garden.

I suggested to Don that we go out into the rock garden and have lunch. About midway of the river, we found a flat rock about the size of a coffee table on which to spread our lunch. About the time we were removing the lunch from the ice chest, I heard a splash of water. Then I noticed a small amount of water lap upon a rock. When I raised my eyes from the bottom of the river, I was shocked to see a wall of water about 12 feet tall within 10 to 15 feet from us, reaching from bank to bank . . . a distance of about 400 feet.

I screamed, "Don, the river is rising!" (Big understatement.) I had made two steps toward the bank when the wall of water hit me. For several minutes I was tumbling, head over heels, in the cascading water. In trying to communicate with Don, I received water in the lungs and stomach. In my mind, I prayed that my head would not hit a rock and knock me unconscious. I could not reach the surface to even attempt to get air.

Suddenly I became aware that I was in a hydraulic whirlpool upside down. My feet were swirling in a large circle and my head and arms in a small tight circle, all while I was being pumped up and down. I tried to swim with the swirl and, when that failed, against the swirl to reach the surface. When that didn't work, I accepted the fact that this was the end of the road for me.

I had three anxieties: 1) concern as to whether Don had drowned, 2) that I would not see my family again, and 3) that I would not see my church family again on this side. Right after these three anxieties, when the yellow water began to turn black, I prayed my final prayer, "Lord I am a dead man if you do not rescue me." Then I was totally gone.

Strange as it may seem, on the other side I was floating downstream in a beautiful river, and both banks were covered with gorgeous flowers of many, many colors. There were colors there that did not seem to exist on Earth, or was it simply that my vision had been perfected? Later, the best we could calculate, I seemed to have been in the drowned state about 20 minutes. At the end of this time, I was suddenly conscious again, hanging upside down in a 4-foot-wide tunnel of air that reached from the surface of the water to the riverbed. The water seemed to be churning behind a glass wall.

Then I thought, "I am defying gravity." At this moment a hand came from my right side and was placed at the navel. Then a left hand was placed at the small of my back. Instantly, I saw an angel at my right side and I knew I was in his hands. He appeared to be about

20 feet tall, if his feet were on the river bottom. He flipped me, gently, right side up, and released me on the surface of the water. I was still about 40 feet from the bank, which was covered with sycamore trees.

My efforts to swim to the bank were futile due to the rough, cascading water. I said a prayer of confession, "Lord, I am not getting a foot closer to the bank." I then again felt the angel's hand, this time against the bottom of my feet, and I shot across the water like an arrow out of a bow, making a gentle landing in the sycamore limbs.

I looked around, searching for Don upriver, then across the river, and then down the river. I saw him land in the tree limbs about 50 yards below me. Don yelled above the roar of the river asking five times if I was all right. (In reality, what he was really asking was whether I was truly alive because he had surfaced three times and each time had seen my feet breaking the surface of the water as the whirlpool pumped me up and down.)

Then we pushed ourselves through the brush to a guardrail where we had a genuine thanksgiving prayer meeting. Our shoes, wallets, and keys were still with us. As we walked back up the riverbank to the camper, Don asked me five more times if I was all right. The repetition was probably a result of our deep shock. The first shock was the wall of water that came upon us; then we were in shock that we survived—only by the grace of God.

Back at the camper, we changed into dry clothes and shoes. Then Don said something that should have been humorous, but the circumstances were too serious. He said, "Frank, I had better drive, since you are in deep shock." After asking me 10 times if I was all right, he thought I was the only one in shock.

We departed the park area for Chattanooga, stopping 10 miles down the road for hot tea and coffee. While drinking the hot drinks, Don was staring at me across the table. I asked him why he was staring at me. He said, "I just want to see what a man who has risen from the dead looks like." That was our first time to laugh.

We spent the night at Kay Arthur's place with friends. When we related what had happened to us, we learned that our hostess, Carol, had once experienced the same powerful whirlpool while whitewater rafting.

The next day we stopped in Meridian to have coffee. While there, we were compelled to drive 6 miles out to the lake to see our friends, Bill and Stella. When we entered the house, Stella said, "Frank, the Lord quickened Psalm 18 to me five days ago. I have read it over and over and can't get the message."

I said, "Read it to us." When she reached the 16th verse, we knew that it pertained to our miracle in the river: "He sent from above, he took me, he drew me out of many waters." Stella had not even known that we were on a trip. Does this not confirm that there is a heavenly joining among the saints in the church family that bonds us together in safety and security?

I desired to know who the angel was who had rescued us from the river, but I felt that I could not ask until the Father's time. Eight months later in Stoneboro, Pa., while alone upstairs in the parsonage, the presence of the Lord suddenly flooded the room. In that presence, I felt liberty to ask who the angel was. The Lord answered that it had been "the angel of my presence that I sent with Moses to deliver my people, Israel, from the Egyptian bondage, who also parted the waters of the Red Sea" (Ex. 33:14-17). You can imagine that my heart soared at the answer.

I learned later that the angel also had placed his hand against Don's feet to catapult him across the troubled waters. (We found out that this event happened 3 miles below a hydroelectric dam in the area of the Tennessee Valley Authority. It was the rainy season; the lake had become too full of water, so they opened the gates and released the river on us.)

Yours in Christ,
Frank Crawford

FAITH VISIT OUTLINE

Preparation

INTRODUCTION
INTERESTS
INVOLVEMENT
    Church Experience/Background
        Ask about the person's church background.
        Listen for clues about the person's spiritual involvement.
    Sunday School Testimony
        Tell general benefits of Sunday School.
        Tell a current personal experience.
    Evangelistic Testimony
        Tell a little of your pre-conversion experience.
        Say: "I had a life-changing experience."
        Tell recent benefits of your conversion.

INQUIRY
Key Question: In your personal opinion, what do you understand it takes for a person to go to heaven?
    Possible answers: Faith, works, unclear, no opinion
Transition Statement: I'd like to share with you how the Bible answers this question, if it is all right. There is a word that can be used to answer this question: FAITH (*spell out on fingers*).

Presentation

F is for FORGIVENESS
We cannot have eternal life and heaven without God's forgiveness.
    "*In Him [meaning Jesus] we have redemption through His blood, the forgiveness of sins*" – Ephesians 1:7a, NKJV.

A is for AVAILABLE
Forgiveness is available. It is –
AVAILABLE FOR ALL
    "*For God so loved the world that He gave His only begotten*

Son, that whoever believes in Him should not perish but have everlasting life" – John 3:16, NKJV.
BUT NOT AUTOMATIC
"Not everyone who says to Me, 'Lord, Lord,' shall enter the kingdom of heaven" – Matthew 7:21a, NKJV.

I is for IMPOSSIBLE
It is impossible for God to allow sin into heaven.
GOD IS –
LOVE
John 3:16, NKJV
JUST
"For judgment is without mercy" – James 2:13a, NKJV.
MAN IS SINFUL
"For all have sinned and fall short of the glory of God" – Romans 3:23, NKJV.

Question: But how can a sinful person enter heaven, where God allows no sin?

T is for TURN
Question: If you were driving down the road and someone asked you to turn, what would he or she be asking you to do? (Change direction.)
Turn means repent.
TURN from something – sin and self
"But unless you repent you will all likewise perish" – Luke 13:3b, NKJV.
TURN to someone; trust Christ only
(The Bible tells us that) "Christ died for our sins according to the Scriptures, and that He was buried, and that He rose again the third day according to the Scriptures" – 1 Corinthians 15:3b-4, NKJV.
"If you confess with your mouth the Lord Jesus and believe in your heart that God has raised Him from the dead, you will be saved" – Romans 10:9, NKJV.

H is for HEAVEN
Heaven is eternal life.
HERE
> "I have come that they may have life, and that they may have it more abundantly" – John 10:10b, NKJV.

HEREAFTER
> "And if I go and prepare a place for you, I will come again and receive you to Myself; that where I am, there you may be also" – John 14:3, NKJV.

HOW
How can a person have God's forgiveness, heaven and eternal life, and Jesus as personal Savior and Lord? Explain based on leaflet picture, FAITH (**F**orsaking **A**ll **I** **T**rust **H**im), Romans 10:9.

Invitation

INQUIRE
Understanding what we have shared, would you like to receive this forgiveness by trusting in Christ as your personal Savior and Lord?

INVITE
    Pray to accept Christ.
    Pray for commitment/recommitment.
    Invite to join Sunday School.

INSURE
Use *A Step of Faith* to insure decision
    Personal Acceptance
    Sunday School Enrollment
    Public Confession

Used with permission.

EVANGECUBE®
(O CUBO EVANGELÍSTICO)
UNFOLDING THE ANSWER TO LIFE'S GREATEST PUZZLE!
(¡DESCUBRIENDO LA RESPUESTA AL PRINCIPAL ROMBECABEZAS DE LA VIDA!)

(English)
How to Lead Someone to Jesus Christ Using the EvangeCube

(Use the arrows on the cube to help you see how to open the pictures!)

1 ⇨⇨ Show 'Man in Sin' separated from 'God'

- This light (point to the right side) represents God.
- God is perfect and without sin.
- God loves us!
- God doesn't want us to perish, but to have everlasting life.
- But our sins must be removed in order to have eternal life with God.
- This figure (point to the left side) represents every person — like you and me.
- The darkness represents our sin.
- Sin is anything that God tells us not to do.
- The Bible says "all have sinned and fall short of the glory of God." *(Rom. 3:23)*
- Our sins separate us from God.

2 ⇨⇨ Open to 'Christ on the Cross'

- God loved us so much that He sent His only Son Jesus Christ to earth as a man.
- God made Jesus die on a cross to pay for our sins with His blood. He took our sins in His body on the cross so that we could come to God *(1 Peter 2:24; 3:18).*
- The Bible also says that "God so loved the world that He gave His one and only Son Jesus, that whoever believes in Him shall not perish, but have everlasting life." *(John 3:16)*
- The Bible says, "God demonstrates His own love for us, in that while we were still sinners, Christ died for us." *(Romans 5:8)*

3 ⇨⇨ Open to the 'Tomb'   **4 ⇩ Open to 'Risen Christ'**

- Men buried Jesus in a tomb.
- They rolled a huge stone in front of it.
- Soldiers guarded the tomb.
- God sent an angel to roll away the big stone and scare away the soldiers.
- God raised Jesus from the dead!
- Soon afterward, God took Jesus back to heaven.
- Jesus has paid the price for our sin, and Jesus has conquered death.

5 ⇨⇨ Open to 'Cross Bridge'

- Jesus is the only way we can come to God.
- Jesus said in the Bible, "I am the way, and the truth, and the life; no one comes to the Father [God] except through Me." *(John 14:6)*
- Through Jesus, we can be forgiven of all our sins and be with God forever.
- But just knowing about these things is not enough! We must choose to put our faith in Jesus — to trust in Him to save us from sin.
- If you do not trust in Jesus, then your sins are not removed! *(Hebrews 4:2)*

6 ⇨⇨ Open to 'Heaven & Hell'

- The Bible says that whoever believes in Jesus has eternal life and is not judged. But whoever does not believe in Jesus has been judged already and the wrath of God remains upon him" *(John 3:16, 18, 36).*
- The penalty for sin is death, but eternal life through Jesus is a free gift from God.
- What choice will you make?
- Trust in Jesus Christ to be forgiven and have eternal life? (point to 'heaven')
- Or reject Jesus Christ and suffer eternal punishment in fire? (point to 'hell')

ASK THE QUESTION:
Would you like to trust Jesus right now and be saved?
(if YES, continue)

(Español)
Cómo guiar a alguien a Jesuristo usando el Cubo Evangelístico

(¡Use las flechas que aparecen en el cubo para ayudarle a ver cómo abrir las láminas!)

1 ⇨⇨ Muestre 'Hombre en Pecado' separado de 'Dios'

- Esta luz (señale el lado derecho) representa a Dios.
- Dios es perfecto y sin pecado.
- ¡Dios nos ama!
- Dios no quiere que ninguno de nosotros se pierda sino que tengamos vida eterna.
- Pero se le debe dar una solución al problema del pecado a fin de tener la vida eterna con Dios.
- Esta figura (señale el lado izquierdo) representa a cada persona – usted y yo.
- La oscuridad representa nuestro pecado.
- Pecado es cualquier cosa que Dios dice que no debemos hacer.
- La Biblia dice que "todos pecaron, y están destituidos de la gloria de Dios" *(Rom. 3:23).*
- Nuestros pecados nos separan de Dios.

2 ⇨⇨ Abra hacia 'Cristo en la cruz'

- Dios nos amó tanto que envió al mundo a su único Hijo Jesucristo en forma de hombre.
- Jesús murió en la cruz para pagar por nuestros pecados con su sangre. Él cargó nuestros pecados en su cuerpo en la cruz para que pudiéramos llegar a Dios *(1 Pedro 2:24; 3:18).*
- La Biblia dice: "Mas Dios muestra su amor para con nosotros, en que siendo aún pecadores, Cristo murió por nosotros" *(Romanos 5:8).*
- La Biblia también dice: "Porque de tal manera amó Dios al mundo, que ha dado a su Hijo unigénito, para que todo aquel que en él cree, no se pierda, mas tenga vida eterna" *(Juan 3:16).*

3 ⇨⇨ Abra hacia 'la tumba'   **4 ⇩ Abra hacia 'Cristo resucitado'**

- Los hombres sepultaron a Jesús en una tumba.
- Ellos pusieron una enorme piedra para cerrar el sepulcro.
- Soldados estaban vigilando.
- Dios envió a un ángel para que corriera la gran piedra y asustara a los soldados.
- ¡Dios resucitó a Jesús de entre los muertos!
- Poco después, Dios llevó a Jesús de regreso al cielo.
- Jesús ha pagado el precio por nuestro pecado, y ha vencido a la muerte.

5 ⇨⇨ Abra hacia 'El puente de la cruz'

- Jesús es el único camino por el que podemos llegar a Dios.
- Jesús dijo en la Biblia: "Yo soy el camino, y la verdad, y la vida; nadie viene al Padre, sino por mí" *(Juan 14:6).*
- A través de Jesús, podemos tener el perdón de todos nuestros pecados y estar con Dios para siempre.
- ¡Pero solamente saber estas cosas no es suficiente! Debemos decidir poner nuestra fe en Jesús – confiar en él para que nos salve de nuestros pecados.
- Si tú no das este paso de poner tu confianza en Jesucristo, tus pecados no se eliminan! *(Hebreos 4:2).*

6 ⇨⇨ Abra hacia 'Cielo e infierno'

- La Biblia dice que quien cree en Jesús tiene vida eterna y no es condenado. ¡Pero quien no cree en Jesús ya ha sido condenado y la ira de Dios está sobre esa persona! *(Juan 3:16, 18, 36).*
- El castigo por el pecado es muerte, pero la vida eterna a través de Jesús es un regalo gratuito de Dios.
- ¿Qué elegirás?
- ¿Confiarás en Jesucristo para ser perdonado y tener la vida eterna? (señale el "cielo")
- ¿O rechazarás a Jesucristo y sufrirás el castigo eterno de fuego? (señale el "infierno")

HAGA LA PREGUNTA:
¿Te gustaría confiar en Jesús ahora mismo y ser salvo?
(si la respuesta es sí, continúe)

1. Man in sin separated from God

This light (point to the right side) represents God. God is perfect and without sin. God loves us! God doesn't want us to perish, but to have everlasting life. But our sins must be removed in order to have eternal life with God. This figure (point to the left side) represents every person like you and me. The darkness represents our sin. Sin is anything that God tells us not to do. The Bible says "all have sinned and fall short of the glory of God." (Rom. 3:23). Our sins separate us from God.

2. Christ on the cross

God loved us so much that He sent His only Son Jesus Christ to earth as a man. God made Jesus die on a cross to pay for our sins with His blood. He took our sins in His body on the cross so that we could come to God (1 Peter 2:24, 3:18). The Bible also says that "God so loved the world that He gave His one and only Son [Jesus], that whoever believes in Him shall not perish, but have everlasting life" (John 3:16). The Bible says, "God demonstrates His own love for us, in that while we were still sinners, Christ died for us"(Romans 5:8).

3. The tomb

Men buried Jesus in a tomb. They rolled a huge stone in front of it. Soldiers guarded the tomb.

4. Risen Christ

God sent an angel to roll away the big stone and scare away the soldiers. God raised Jesus from the dead! Soon afterward, God took Jesus back to heaven. Jesus has paid the price for our sin, and Jesus has conquered death.

5. Cross bridge

Jesus is the only way we can come to God. Jesus said in the Bible, "I am the way, and the truth, and the life; no one comes to the Father [God] except through Me." (John 14:6) Through Jesus, we can be forgiven of all our sins and be with God forever.

6. Heaven and hell

The Bible says that whoever believes in Jesus has eternal life- and is not judged. But whoever does not believe in Jesus has been judged already, and the wrath of God remains upon him! (John 3:16, 18, 36). The penalty for sin is death, but eternal life through Jesus is a free gift from God. What choice will you make? Trust in Jesus Christ to be forgiven and have eternal life? (Point to 'heaven.') Or reject Jesus Christ and suffer eternal punishment in fire? (Point to 'hell.') But just knowing about these things is not enough! We must choose to put our faith in Jesus — to trust in Him to save us from sin. If you do not take the step of trusting in Jesus, then your sins are not removed! (Hebrews 4:2)
ASK THE QUESTION: Would you like to trust Jesus right now and be saved?

7. Steps for followers of Christ

LOVE God and all people. "You shall love the Lord your God with all your heart, and with all your soul, and with all your mind. This is the great and foremost commandment. And a second is like it: you shall love your neighbor as yourself" (Matt. 22:36-40). STUDY the Bible (God's Word) daily. Start with the Gospel of John; read one chapter each day. "Like newborn babes, long for the pure milk of the word, that by it you may grow in respect to salvation ..." (1 Peter 2:2). "If anyone loves Me, he will keep My word" (John 14:23). PRAY to God constantly. In prayer you can thank and worship God, ask for His help, confess your sins, and pray for others. "Be anxious for nothing, but in everything by prayer and supplication with thanksgiving, let your requests be made known to God" (Phil. 4:6-7). MEET regularly with other Christians. God commands that Christians meet regularly for worship, prayer, Bible study, and helping each other. "...not forsaking our own assembling together, as is the habit of some, but encouraging one another ..."(Heb. 10:25). TELL others the good news about Jesus. God wants us to tell other people how to have eternal life with God by trusting in Jesus to save them from sin. You can use this paper when you talk to others about Jesus! "And He (Jesus) said to them, 'Go into all the world, and preach the gospel to all creation.'" (Mark 16:1).

Used with permission.

What's Important to You?

Not long ago I got a phone call about investing in an oilfield service company. The representative approached me about investing in a new technology that he indicated would be an excellent means to make a significant amount of money, especially with the price of oil these days. I wasn't interested, but he persisted and asked that at I least let him send me some information about the radial jetting technology. I told him he could send it if he wished, as long as he understood I was making no promises.

A week later I got the information. I glanced over it quickly, which was enough to make me strongly suspect it was just another gimmick for one person to make money off someone else's investment.

A couple of days later the rep called back with a really hard pitch, promising the new radial jetting technology made it possible to pump 10 or more barrels of oil a day from old wells that had been producing only one or two barrels per day. Once the wells stabilized at about five barrels daily, they would sell that property, he said, and with the profits buy more old well properties and repeat the process. I told him it sounded awfully good, but I would have to do some research.

We then got into a conversation about what I did. I told him I made a lot of mission trips and that he should buy my book, *You Will Never Run Out of Jesus*. He said he would buy it with a coupon he had with Amazon.com.

I did do a little research about the materials he had sent and decided that the scheme sounded literally too good to be true. So I let it ride.

Soon I was contacted by the marketing manager and got an even harder sell on the project. By this time he had gone so far as to Fed-Ex a form for me to sign for buying into the partnership. When I mentioned that any money I invested would have to come from my IRA, the manager said that my broker might advise me not to invest with them. With that final red flag, I had a clear conscience about not investing with them, particularly after my wife agreed.

A couple of days later, the representative called again and asked why I had not returned the completed paperwork. I told him I had evaluated the business and didn't think it was right for me. Wow! You would have thought I had stabbed him with a knife. He ranted that he had spent too much time with me for me not to respond affirmatively.

I asked what part of "no" he didn't understand. It was like pouring cold water on a cat; I could almost hear the hiss. I heard a loud noise as if he had kicked a filing cabinet. Then I got another lecture about what a great deal this was and how he couldn't believe that I did not care about making a lot of money. I remained adamant and finally told him I had to go as company had arrived. I hung up.

Immediately he called back — and then he called back again. I didn't answer the phone. Two hours later he called yet again. It had become a battle of wills. When I picked up the phone, he proceeded to give me yet another sales pitch. I think I must have been the first person to ever tell him no. He gave his history of how he had succeeded in business. Then he challenged me, asking what the most important thing was that I had ever done. I did not hesitate to tell him. It's when I tell others about the saving grace of Jesus Christ, I said, and they accept him as Savior. *Silence.*

I asked him if he was a Christian and got a short *yes*. Then I asked him if he knew what it took to go to heaven. I even offered him a clue: I told him there was only one ticket to get there. He said he would have to think about that. Then he offered a long list of what he considered were his good works. It was far from a faith answer. I proceeded to tell him that the one and only ticket to heaven is belief in the Lord Jesus Christ. For the first time, amazingly, he was subdued. Finally, he said he had to go; he had a meeting to attend.

The entire episode reminded me all too well of the dissatisfaction and sadness that result when we make money into a god. I believe the best life I can ever lead is one in which I have the courage to tell others about that which is truly the most important thing we can ever do, and that is live for Jesus.

CrossHouse

P.O. Box 461592
Garland, TX 75046

1-877-212-3022 (Office)
1-888-252-3022 (Fax)

ORDER MORE COPIES OF
There's Something Better Than Going to Heaven
BY PHONE, FAX or MAIL

Date: _____
Bill to: _____

Order#: _____
Ship to: _____

Phone: _____

Card # _____
Exp. date: _____

Signature: _____

Item	Quantity	Price	Total
There's Something Better Than Going to Heaven		$9.95	
Sales Tax (8.25%) Texas Residents Only			
Shipping ($3 for first book, 50 cents for each addtl.)			
		Grand Total	

Printed in the United States
200402BV00002B/304-657/A